GUIDE TO UNDERSTANDING ANNUITIES

CONTENTS

- **2** Planning for Retirement Income
- **4** The Possibilities of Annuities
- **6** Nonqualified Annuities
- **8** Fixed Annuities
- **10** Variable Annuities
- **12** More about Variable Annuities
- **14** Annuity Income
- **16** Immediate Annuity Income
- **18** Understanding Variable Income
- **20** Converting to Income
- **22** Annuitization Options
- **24** Annuitization Strategy
- **26** What You Pay
- **28** More about Fees
- **30** Taxing Annuity Income
- **32** Glossary

ANNUITIES

Planning for Retirement Income

Retiring means stitching together different sources of income.

When you retire, you'll share a common experience with everyone who has already made the change: You won't take home a paycheck anymore.

Without this steady stream of revenue, you'll have to establish a financial plan that provides for the income you'll need to live on. Specifically, you'll need to consider:

- What sources of income are you confident you can count on?
- How much income will they provide each year?
- How and when will the income be paid?
- How will you coordinate payments from different sources to create a steady stream of income, so that there's money in the bank when you need it?

WHAT THE SOURCES ARE

Your retirement income may come from a variety of sources.

Social Security is lifetime income paid to people who have participated in the system and to their surviving spouses.

Defined benefit pensions are designed to provide lifetime income from a plan your employer creates and funds.

Defined contribution plans, such as 401(k) plans, are designed to provide income from investment earnings on tax-deferred contributions made by you or your employer or both.

IRAs are tax-deferred or tax-free individual retirement accounts. You contribute earned income to produce investment earnings that you can withdraw as retirement income.

Annuities are fixed or variable insurance company products that allow you to convert your premiums and any tax-deferred earnings to lifetime income.

Personal investments in taxable accounts can provide interest, dividends, and capital gains as retirement income or can be sold if you need cash.

Jobs can provide income if you want to work and work is available.

WHEN THE MONEY ARRIVES

Unlike a paycheck, which arrives regularly, retirement income arrives on different schedules. Social Security checks and annuity and pension payments usually come monthly. Others, like stock dividends, arrive quarterly. Interest on many bonds is paid semi-annually. Few, if any payments, are weekly or biweekly. That means you have to think about balancing the amount coming in to meet your expenses.

ANNUITIES

PUTTING IT TOGETHER

Managing your finances during retirement involves juggling your sources of income to make sure you have enough money to live on. It's a lot like making a quilt: No piece by itself is big enough to keep you warm at night. But properly stitched together, the pieces may provide the comfort you'd like to have.

THE BIGGER PICTURE

The regular income you can expect from Social Security and a defined benefit pension depends on your work history. In general, the longer you work and the higher your salary, the more income you can anticipate, up to the annual ceilings.

Realistically, though, neither of these sources is likely to be as important a source of retirement income in the future as they have in the past. Social Security faces the imbalance of more beneficiaries and fewer workers, and fewer employers are offering defined benefit plans.

The retirement income you can expect from other potential sources depends on three things: how much is invested, where it's invested, and the long-term return those investments provide. You have much greater control over these choices, and so much greater responsibility for the outcome than you may realize.

That's why it's critical to put basic investment principles to work, including asset allocation and diversification, across your tax-deferred as well as your taxable portfolios. It's also why you want to start thinking seriously about retirement income before you start thinking seriously about retiring.

TURNING INVESTMENTS INTO INCOME

One of the challenges you face in managing retirement income is that net worth doesn't translate directly into income that you can use to pay your bills or make new investments. Stocks may pay dividends, but much of their value is the price per share you could realize only if you sold. You can spend bond interest, but if you liquidate the bond when it matures rather than reinvesting that amount, you won't earn interest in the future.

On the other hand, you must take regular cash distributions from your tax-deferred retirement accounts once you reach 70½. To meet that requirement—and create a cash flow—you might establish a systematic withdrawal schedule, or, in the case of an annuity contract, choose annuitization. That means converting your account value to a lifetime income stream.

One approach is to spread your retirement savings around among a number of products and accounts, each designed to fill a different role. That might mean putting some money in stocks, some in bonds, some in mutual funds, some in real estate, and some in fixed or variable annuities or both.

ANNUITIES
The Possibilities of Annuities

You decide on the annuity features that put you on the right track.

Annuities are insurance company contracts. The premiums you pay and tax-deferred earnings on those premiums are designed to be a source of retirement income, either in the future if you choose a **deferred annuity** or right away with an **immediate annuity**.

With a deferred annuity, the principal and earnings accumulate in the build-up period. Eventually you can **annuitize**, which means you convert your account value to a stream of lifetime income, or you can take the money some other way. With an immediate annuity, the lifetime income you receive is based on several factors including the amount of your purchase, your age, and the interest rate.

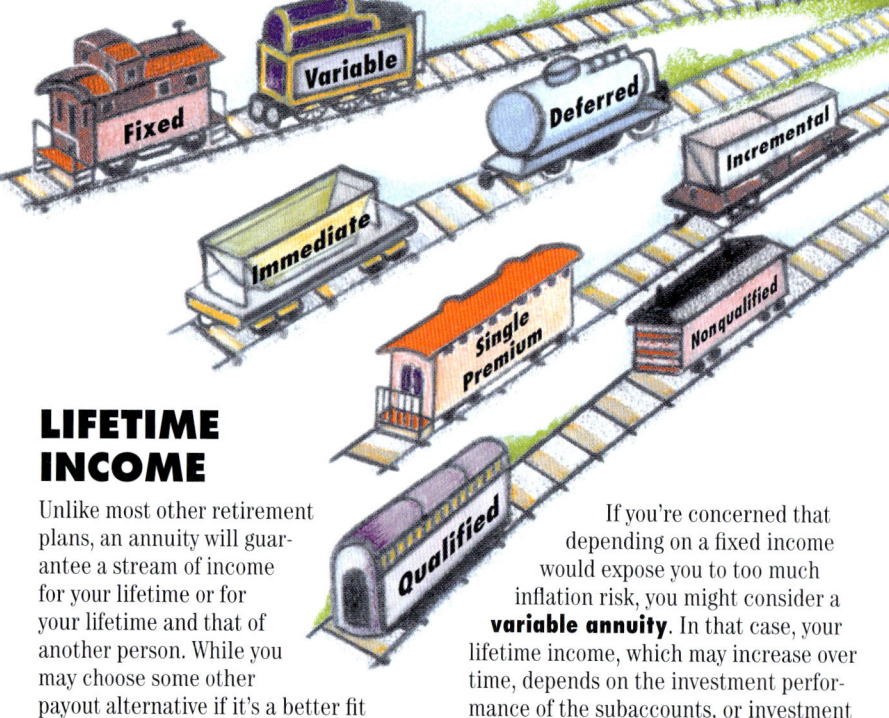

LIFETIME INCOME

Unlike most other retirement plans, an annuity will guarantee a stream of income for your lifetime or for your lifetime and that of another person. While you may choose some other payout alternative if it's a better fit with your long-term financial plan, the assurance of income for life can help make your retirement more secure.

For example, if your **fixed annuity** pays you a specific amount each month for your lifetime, your finances may not be as vulnerable to losses in the investment markets, which may reduce your dividend or interest income or eat into your principal. Remember, though, that fixed annuity income depends on the ability of the issuing company to pay, so researching annuity company ratings before buying is crucial.

If you're concerned that depending on a fixed income would expose you to too much inflation risk, you might consider a **variable annuity**. In that case, your lifetime income, which may increase over time, depends on the investment performance of the subaccounts, or investment funds, you select from among those offered in the contract. The risks in this case are the potential for a decrease in income in some periods and loss of capital.

ANNUITIES

QUALIFIED OR NONQUALIFIED?

If you participate in a retirement plan where you work, you may find that your employer includes a fixed or variable annuity, or both, in the menu of plan choices. When annuity contracts are offered through a **qualified plan** they are considered **qualified annuities**. In this case, qualified means subject to the federal rules that govern how the plans are operated.

Money you contribute to a qualified annuity reduces your current taxable salary in addition to accumulating tax-deferred earnings. But you must begin required withdrawals no later than 70½ and take at least the required minimum each year.

Alternately—or in addition—you can buy an annuity that's not offered through a qualified plan. In this case, the contract is a **nonqualified annuity**. Among the key differences are that you pay the premiums with after-tax dollars, you can contribute more than the federal limit for qualified plans, and you can postpone taking income until much later in your life if you wish.

THE WAY YOU PAY

You can buy an annuity with a **single premium** or make payments over time, on either a regular or discretionary schedule. Your payment alternatives are spelled out in the contract you sign. Immediate annuities, for example, are typically single premium purchases while contributions to a qualified annuity are made over time.

Unlike **individual retirement accounts (IRAs)**, to which you must contribute earned income, you can buy a nonqualified annuity with unearned income. For example, if you sell a business, gain an inheritance, or receive an insurance settlement, you could use that money to buy a single premium contract.

Within a variable nonqualified annuity, you can move your assets among different funds during the accumulation period without owing income tax on any gains, as you can within an IRA or qualified retirement plan. There may be a fee for moving assets out of certain types of funds, though, or for transfers over the limit the contract allows.

THE ANNUITY DEBATE

Annuities, variable annuities in particular, have advocates and critics. The advocates feel that the insurance protection the contracts offer, the potential for growth, and promise of lifetime income make them valuable retirement planning products. Critics argue that annuity fees are too high for the investment and insurance benefits these contracts provide.

ANNUITIES

Nonqualified Annuities

You can buy a nonqualified annuity for your personal retirement portfolio.

If you are saving for retirement, a **nonqualified annuity** offers the benefits of tax-deferred earnings during the accumulation period and the option of receiving lifetime income if you annuitize your contract. As with other tax-deferred savings, there is usually a penalty for withdrawing from an annuity or ending your contract before you're at least 59½—though there are some exceptions. The timing on mandatory withdrawals varies, depending on the type of nonqualified annuity you buy and where you live.

THE RANGE OF CHOICES
Nonqualified annuities come in many flavors. You can choose a contract that has no annual contribution limits and purchase it with money from any source, including a gift or inheritance. You can buy an annuity within a conventional individual retirement account (IRA). Or, you can open a traditional or Roth IRA with an annuity provider. Then IRA stands for **individual retirement annuity**. With any type of IRA annuity, the annual contribution limit applies and you must buy with earned income.

You can select either a fixed or variable contract as a nonqualified annuity. You can purchase two contracts, one fixed and the other variable. Or you can include a fixed track within a variable annuity contract.

THE USES THEY SERVE
You might purchase a nonqualified annuity to supplement the amount you're putting into an employer sponsored plan or, if you're self-employed, use a nonqualified annuity as a secondary source of retirement income.

Most financial advisers suggest that you invest the maximum allowed in your employer sponsored plan before contributing to a nonqualified annuity.

But because annuities may offer greater variety and flexibility than investments you can make in some employer plans, using them may be a way to diversify your portfolio. For example, if you're part of a plan that puts your pension money into company stock, you might use a nonqualified annuity to put money into other types of equity portfolios. Or if your defined benefit plan will pay you a fixed amount after you retire, you might put money into a variable nonqualified annuity that provides an opportunity for your annuity income to outpace inflation.

YOU'RE THE BOSS
The federal government doesn't require you to begin withdrawing from your standalone or Roth IRA nonqualified annuities

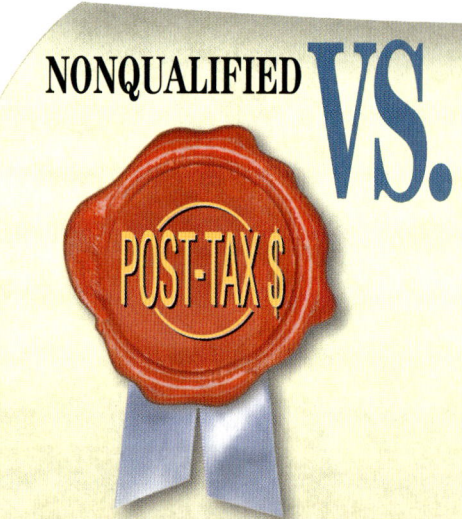

NONQUALIFIED VS. POST-TAX $

Post-tax, or after-tax, dollars are what's left of your earnings after taxes are taken out. Contributions to nonqualified retirement plans are made with after-tax dollars. When you eventually take money out of nonqualified plans, you don't owe tax on the portion of the withdrawal that's considered return of principal. It has already been paid.

WAYS THEY'RE ALIKE
Tax-deferred earnings

Early withdrawal penalty

WAYS THEY'RE DIFFERENT
Invest after-tax dollars

No contribution limits

Income from any source

Flexible withdrawal rules

ANNUITIES

COMPANY RULES
Under the terms of most nonqualified annuity contracts, insurance companies require you to begin withdrawals by a certain age such as 85 or 90, or even later, though you don't need to wait that long.

QUALIFIED ANNUITIES

Pretax dollars are what you earn before federal and state taxes are deducted. When contributions to qualified retirement plans are made with pretax dollars, it reduces the current income tax you owe because your taxable income is reduced by the amount you invest. Eventually, though, you owe taxes both on the investment and the earnings when you take money out of the plan.

Tax-deferred earnings

Early withdrawal penalty

Invest pretax dollars

Contribution limits

Earned income only

Required withdrawal rules

when you turn 70½, as you must with a traditional IRA and many qualified retirement plans. Some states have no age requirement for annuity withdrawals either, while others impose mandatory withdrawals at some point, generally much later than 70½.

MAKING CHANGES
If you want to move your nonqualified annuity assets to another annuity with a different company, you can do that with a tax-free transfer known as a 1035 exchange. You may also be able to arrange a tax-free transfer of assets in a variable annuity to a fixed annuity, or vice versa.

While you don't owe tax on any account earnings at the time of the transfer, you might owe surrender charges on the contract you're leaving and be subject to a new surrender period under the new contract. Other charges may apply as well.

In contrast, if you moved assets in a mutual fund from one fund family to another, you would owe capital gains taxes on any increase in value unless you owned the funds in a tax-deferred or tax-free account.

AN ANNUITY DEBATE
Some people question buying variable annuities in an IRA, since an annuity in an IRA does not provide any additional tax-deferred advantage beyond that provided by the IRA itself. These people maintain that you are adding a layer of additional fees to your IRA, which could make it harder to achieve the same return as you might otherwise earn, assuming you allocated your money in similar ways.

On the other hand, mortality and expense risk (M&E) and other fees pay for features including the guaranteed death benefit and the option of lifetime income. You should weigh the cost of these features, and the annuity's investment choices, when you consider whether or not to include a variable annuity in your IRA portfolio.

ROTH IRAS
Roth IRAs, in which you invest after-tax dollars, can provide tax-free retirement income if your account has been open at least five years and you're at least 59½ when you withdraw. Your contribution is limited to the annual IRA cap and you must have an adjusted gross income of less than $110,000 if you're single or $160,000 if you're married and file a joint return to be eligible to contribute.

If you should die before you begin to collect income from a variable annuity, your beneficiary can be paid a death benefit based on your premiums and, in some contracts, on your earnings.

Since collecting on the guarantee depends on the annuity provider's ability to pay claims, you should research the issuing company's ratings and financial strength before you buy.

ANNUITIES

Fixed Annuities

Traditional annuities earn a fixed rate of interest and pay a fixed income.

When you buy a **fixed deferred annuity** contract, you get two promises from the issuer: a fixed rate of return during the **accumulation**, or **build-up, period** while your retirement savings compound, and many ways to receive retirement income, including payments that are guaranteed to continue for as long as you live.

The two promises are related. Your money in the annuity grows tax deferred until you're ready to withdraw. The earnings rate paid on your savings, the amount you save, and the length of time your annuity grows all determine the income you'll receive. For many people, the certainty of a fixed rate of return is a chief attraction of fixed annuities.

The rate you're paid is guaranteed for the period stated in the contract, whether interest rates move up or down. But you may face surrender charges if you end your contract early.

BUILD UP

SETTING THE RATE
The company that issues the annuity sets the **current rate** of interest it will pay on its contract with you and revises it periodically. Rates may be adjusted monthly, annually, or less frequently. When the rate changes, it sometimes increases and sometimes decreases, reflecting what's happening in the economy at large. But it can never go below the **guaranteed rate**, the state-mandated minimum that's set when you buy the annuity.

In general, the new rate is based on the return the company is earning on its own investment portfolio, typically government and corporate bonds and residential mortgages. The **spread**, or difference between what the issuing company expects to earn and what it commits itself to pay out, can help offset some of its expenses and provide some of its profits.

You can comparison shop for earning potential as well as for high ratings and financial strength of the insurance company providing the annuity. The fact that renewal interest rates tend to be lower than introductory, or first year rates, can complicate your comparison of earning potential. One solution is to compare older policies as well as the new ones offered by the same insurance companies.

Current Rate

Guaranteed Rate

A SECOND CHANCE
Fixed annuities can have a **bailout clause**, sometimes known as an escape clause, that lets you surrender your policy without penalty if the interest rate that's being offered drops below a certain level, often one percentage point less than the previous rate, even if it's above the guaranteed rate.

There are a couple of catches though:

Usually if an annuity's rate drops significantly, interest rates in general have dropped. That means newly issued annuities are likely to be paying at comparable levels to the one you're giving up.

And if you transfer your money to a different type of investment or keep the cash, and you're younger than 59½, you may have to pay a 10% premature with

ANNUITIES

HOW COMPANIES INVEST

The amount you invest to buy a fixed annuity contract goes into the provider's general account, along with premiums from other investors and other company revenues. Because the company has such large sums to invest, it can diversify its holdings and earn a better return on its investment than you could investing on your own, taking the same investment risk.

A potential downside to buying a fixed annuity may occur if the issuing company gets into financial difficulties, since its creditors have a right to assets in the general account. These situations are highly unlikely, however, since the insurance industry is heavily regulated and individual companies are rated regularly.

But be alert: Companies touting fixed annuity returns much higher than the rates offered by the competition may be too good to be true. Sometimes, promises of stellar returns are a red flag that annuity money is going into riskier investments, like junk bonds. Before buying, ask to see the rate that the issuing company has paid over the past ten years and be sure to check the company's ratings.

COMPARATIVE RATES

The more competitive the annuity market, the greater the likelihood that the interest rates on the plans you're considering will be attractive. Typically, the rates are on a par with what you'd earn on a long-term bond, and higher than what CDs and money market funds are paying.

PAY OUT

SAFETY FIRST

Fixed annuities, sometimes called guaranteed annuities, are considered safe because you can count on receiving the specific return you're promised each year.

The guarantee is backed by the insurance company issuing the annuity, not the government. But if you buy your contract from a highly rated company, its financial strength and reputation stand behind your contract.

Rating services such as Standard & Poor's, Moody's, A.M. Best, and Fitch rank annuity providers on their overall financial condition, which underlies their ability to meet their obligations. These reports are available in public libraries, on the Internet, from your financial adviser, and from the insurance company if you request it.

THE INFLATION ISSUE

The flip side of safety, or the guaranteed return, is that the income you receive does not increase with inflation the way that Social Security payments do. The major risk of any fixed income source is that your costs will increase over time, but the income you receive will not.

If inflation should increase rapidly, as it sometimes does, an income that was once adequate may leave you short of cash. And the longer you live and continue to collect, the less far your income is likely to stretch even if inflation increases only modestly.

drawal penalty on your taxable earnings, plus whatever taxes are due. If you withdraw only part of the accumulated contract value, the federal government's rules say that you withdraw earnings first, not the principal. That means you could pay tax on the entire withdrawal amount.

PROTECTING OTHERS

While you usually buy a fixed annuity to provide retirement income for yourself, or for yourself and your spouse, you can also purchase an annuity to provide lifetime income for another person whom you support, such as an elderly relative or a disabled child.

ANNUITIES

Variable Annuities

Variable annuities offer investors more choices.

Variable annuities have many of the same features as fixed annuities—including tax-deferred earnings and a choice of payouts, plus the opportunity to make unlimited contributions if the annuity is nonqualified. In addition, they offer the potential for greater returns and the opportunity to make your own decisions about how to allocate your assets among investment funds offered through your contract.

A potential downside of variable annuities, though, is that the return is not guaranteed. You may have only small gains—or no gains—in some periods and you could lose principal.

CREATING A PORTFOLIO

With variable annuities, lots of things can vary, or change: the rate of return you earn, the amount of income you receive if you **annuitize**, or convert your account value to a stream of income, and how your money is invested.

When you buy a variable annuity, you allocate your premiums among a number of **investment portfolios**, also called **funds, subaccounts**, or **variable accounts**. The accounts may be designed specifically for the annuity company or may be versions of existing funds that are designated for exclusive annuity use. Although the names of the investment portfolios may be the same or similar to those of retail mutual funds, they are not the same funds.

Your job is to choose among the ones that the issuing company offers, much as you would with a 401(k) or 403(b) retirement plan. Typically, there will be a dozen or more, including stock portfolios, a money market account, a government bond portfolio, a corporate bond portfolio, and a guaranteed account, which is similar to a fixed annuity investment. Sometimes, you have an even wider choice drawn from a number of different investment management companies.

MAKING THE INVESTMENT

You can allocate your premiums however you like, usually on a percentage basis: 50% in a growth stock portfolio, for example, 25% in a balanced portfolio, and 25% in a guaranteed or bond account.

Each time you add money, you buy a specific number of **accumulation units**, or shares, based on the **net asset value**

How They Work

1. Choose a variable annuity

(NAV) of the investment portfolio you're putting money into, adjusted for the annuity's mortality and expense risk fee (M&E). The **accumulation unit value** is the current value of the investment portfolio divided by the number of existing accumulation units.

GUARANTEED DEATH BENEFIT

Many investors are attracted by the **death benefit** variable annuities provide, which is based on the claims-paying ability of the insurance company that issues the contract. It means that if you die during the accumulation period, your beneficiaries will receive, at the minimum, the amount you put into the annuity. With most contracts, in fact, investment gains are locked in regularly so that your beneficiaries receive more than your principal, even if the value has dropped at the time of your death below the amount you put into the account. In contrast, a mutual fund pays your beneficiaries whatever your account is worth at the time of your death, even if it's less than the amount you invested.

IN THE BALANCE
You can weigh the advantages of fixed and variable annuities.

Variable	Fixed
Various levels of risk	Guaranteed returns
Greater potential rewards	No inflation protection
Choice of investment portfolios	Insurance company manager chooses investments
Assets in separate accounts	Assets in general accounts

ANNUITIES

THEY'RE YOURS
Variable annuities differ from fixed annuities in another important way. The premiums you allocate to the subaccounts, or investment portfolios, go into individual accounts held in an issuer's **separate account**, rather than into its general account. (The exception is any money you put in a fixed account.) As a result, this part of your retirement savings may be shielded from the issuing company's creditors.

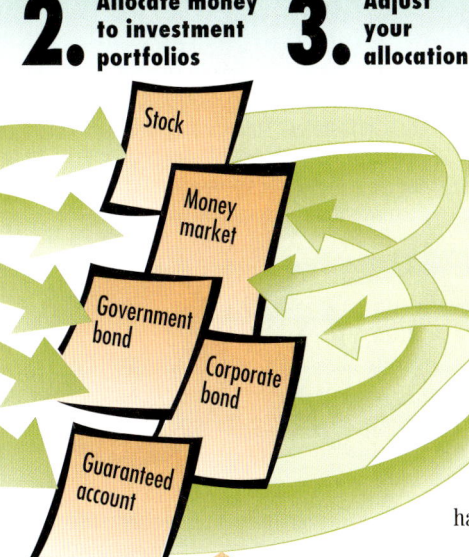

2. Allocate money to investment portfolios

3. Adjust your allocation

4. Receive your payout

UNDERLYING INVESTMENTS
The portfolios you choose in your variable annuity are called your **underlying investments** because the performance of your annuity as a whole is based on how these investment portfolios perform. And the portfolios have underlying investments as well: the stocks or bonds they own. It is the collective performance of those stocks or bonds that determines the performance of the portfolio.

PUTTING MONEY TO WORK
If you purchase a variable annuity by making payments over time, adding a set amount at regular intervals lets you take advantage of **dollar cost averaging (DCA)**. This approach is designed to reduce the risk of trying to choose the best time to buy—though it can't guarantee a profit or protect you against losses.

Because the prices of the underlying investments change regularly, DCA means you purchase a different number of units each time you make a premium payment. Over time, your cost per unit will be less than the average price per unit because you buy more units when the prices are down.

Remember, though, that if you're dollar cost averaging, you must continue to buy annuity units when prices drop in order to reduce your overall cost per unit. If you stop buying in a falling market, you will have paid only the higher prices.

With many variable annuities, you can allocate a specific percentage of your purchase to each of your portfolios as you add money to your account. For example, if you invest $40,000 and have selected four investment portfolios, you might put $10,000 into each of the portfolios. Or, if you invest $400 a month, $100 would go to each of the portfolios.

Another approach is to put the investment amount in a fixed or money market account within the variable annuity and arrange to have the assets moved gradually into one or more of your investment portfolios. Transferring small amounts helps you avoid making a large purchase at what might turn out to be the highest price.

EQUITY INDEXED ANNUITIES
An **equity indexed annuity** lets you benefit from potential gains in the stock market but receive a guaranteed minimum return if the index falls. The basic principle is that the annuity is linked to an index such as the S&P 500. If the index goes up, your account is credited with a return based on a percentage of the gain. If the index falls, your account is credited with the guaranteed return.

One caution is that while the return is based on the performance of the index, you don't get the full boost of a rising market. You'll want to compare participation rates, earnings caps, and surrender charges if you're considering a contract.

ANNUITIES

More about Variable Annuities

You call the shots on allocating your assets with a variable annuity.

Because they provide individual control over retirement savings, variable annuity contracts are more flexible and as a result more complex than fixed contracts. In exchange for giving you more options and choices, they require you to make more decisions.

MANAGING RISK AND RETURN

As with any equity investment, you risk loss of principal with a variable annuity. In some years, you also risk lower returns than you had anticipated. But equity investments also offer greater potential for long-term return and, equally important, better protection against inflation.

The key, of course, is the long-term commitment you make. While it is true that in some periods a fixed annuity might show stronger gains than a stock portfolio, historically the longer that money is in equities, the greater the potential for growth.

Using the principle of **diversification**, you can select investment portfolios that are invested in many different companies and industries. That variety helps protect you against sustained losses in a single stock or sector of the market. What it can't protect you against, however, is a stagnant or falling market in which the majority of equities lose value for an extended period.

BEATING INFLATION

Traditionally, equity investments in variable annuities have out-paced inflation in two ways.

Over time equity investments inside and outside annuities have had stronger returns than other asset classes, though they have lost value in some periods. And

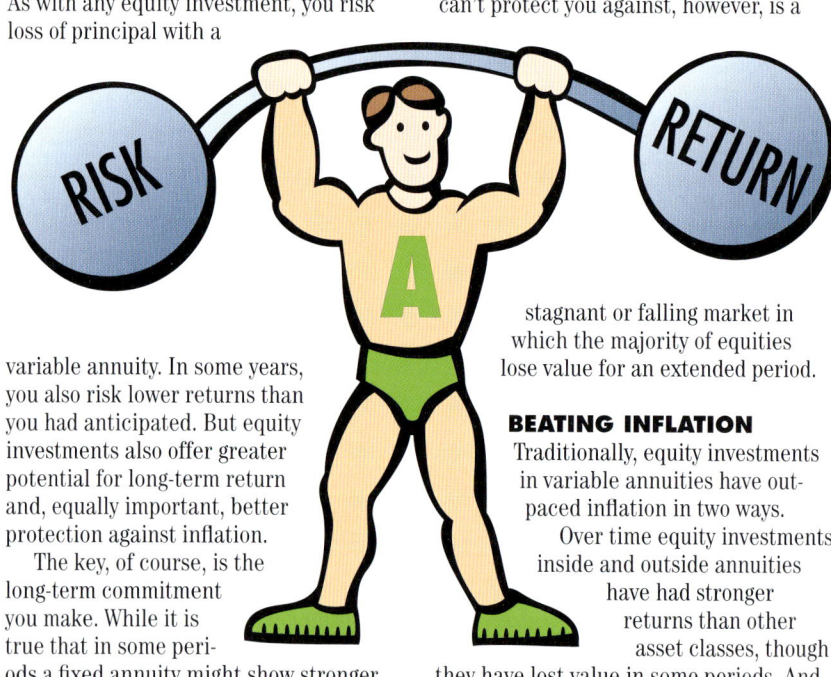

UNDERSTANDING BENCHMARK RATE

If you choose a variable income option when you annuitize, the amount you'll receive is based on an **AIR**, or **assumed interest rate**. It's also referred to as a **hurdle rate** or a **benchmark rate**.

That rate is used to determine the amount of the first income check you receive and is the standard, or benchmark, that's used to determine whether the checks that follow are more or less than the initial one. You may have the option of picking one of two interest rates. At the lower rate, the initial amount is less, but there's the potential for larger payments over time. At the higher rate, the initial amount is larger and you can expect any increases to be more gradual and drops to be more likely.

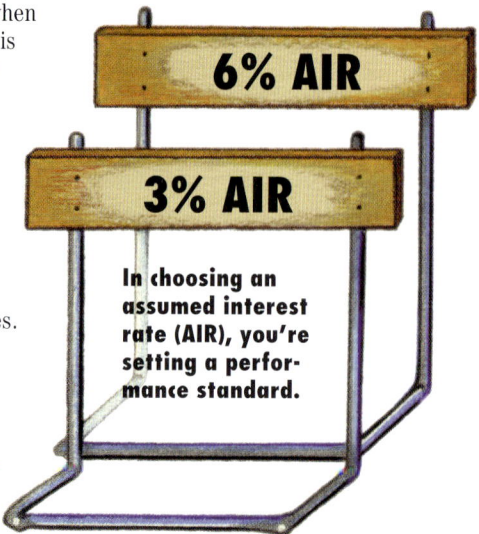

In choosing an assumed interest rate (AIR), you're setting a performance standard.

ANNUITIES

because any annuity earnings are reinvested and no current taxes are due, annuity funds could gain value more quickly than funds earning a comparable rate if money was withdrawn to pay taxes.

Second, with variable annuities you can leave some or all of your retirement savings in growth accounts even after you begin to take income. That means the payments you receive may increase over time—though of course they may also decrease if investment performance slows.

USING BENCHMARKS

If you choose a higher **benchmark rate**, when you **annuitize**, and convert your account value to a stream of income, the amount of your first check will be larger than if you choose a lower rate. If your investment continues to produce the same return after annuity and investment expenses are subtracted (admittedly an unlikely prospect) your annuity income will stay the same. But any change, up or down, in the performance of your investment portfolios means you'll receive different amounts of monthly income over the time you collect. In some variable annuitization plans, the amount is adjusted annually and monthly payments throughout the year remain at the same dollar amount.

Your other choice—the lower benchmark—would produce a smaller initial payment. But you can anticipate larger increases in your monthly income when the performance of your chosen investment portfolios is strong, and you have more protection against a drop in income, since the market return may be less likely to drop below the lower rate.

While committing yourself to a choice such as this may seem difficult, you can ask your investment adviser to track what's happened to variable incomes over the past ten years, and what a sustained drop in the underlying investments would mean to your income.

AN ADDED PLUS

Another major appeal of variable annuities is that you can make tax-free transfers among the portfolios your annuity offers. For example, if you're convinced

INSURANCE GUARANTEES
Part of the cost of owning variable annuities is the insurance protection they provide:
- The guaranteed death benefit to protect beneficiaries against market downturns
- The right to choose a payout option that provides income you can't outlive
- The guarantee that the fee that pays for this insurance will not increase

it's time to increase the percentage of your retirement savings in more aggressive growth stocks, you can shift money from a balanced or money market portfolio. Or you might want to readjust your asset allocation from time to time. This flexibility lets you have continuing control over your retirement savings.

No taxes are due on any gains in your subaccounts when you reallocate within your variable annuity. But there may be a charge if you exceed the number of transfers your contract permits in a calendar year.

MVAs IN VARIABLE ANNUITIES

Sometimes there may be a **market value adjustment (MVA)** on transfers from the fixed-income account of a variable annuity, to adjust for increases and decreases in interest rates. For example, if you wanted to transfer $10,000 from a fixed account to an equity portfolio prior to the maturity date, and after interest rates had gone up, you could move a portion of that amount, and the balance would go to the annuity provider. The terms of each contract can be different, so make sure you check what such an adjustment would be as part of your buying decision.

ANNUITIES

Annuity Income

Annuities exist to provide income in retirement.

You can get annuity income in two ways. You can purchase a **deferred annuity**, typically while you are still working, as a way to help you save for retirement. You determine the amount and frequency of your premiums and when the income will begin, typically in retirement.

Or, you can purchase an **immediate annuity** with a single premium, such as a lump sum payment from a retirement savings plan or the profits from selling your business. As the name implies, immediate annuities begin paying income soon after you purchase the contract.

GROWING MORE FLEXIBLE

The earliest deferred variable annuities offered two choices when you were ready to start receiving income. You could convert your contract to the payout phase, a process called **annuitization**. That generally provided income for as long as you lived but left nothing for your beneficiaries when you died. Or, rather than annuitizing, you could surrender your contract, which meant getting your premiums and earnings back in a lump sum, minus expenses, and owing tax on the earnings. Once you chose, you couldn't change your mind.

Since then, many different annuity payout options have been added that offer greater liquidity and flexibility, even though the basic purpose continues to be to provide retirement income. A variety of payout options is also available with immediate annuities.

For example, many annuity policies now allow you to take a life annuity with a period certain that guarantees payments until the end of the period even if you die before then. And many contracts offer income that continues for a fixed period rather than as long as you live. With some **commutable** contracts, you may be able to accelerate your payments under certain circumstances. That means you can withdraw a lump sum amount after annuitization begins rather than continue to receive regular payments. Though changing your mind may be possible only with certain types of payout plans, the flexibility has real advantages if your life situation changes.

Income Choices

When you're ready to take income, annuity contracts typically offer a number of choices:

- **Lifetime income**

- **Income for a fixed period**

- **Systematic withdrawals**

- **Lump sum withdrawals**

ANNUITIES

FIGHTING INFLATION

Inflation isn't a new topic, and it certainly isn't a pleasant one. If you're living on $50,000 this year, 24 years from now it will cost you $100,000 to live the same way, assuming that the inflation rate stays at its current 3%. If the rate goes up, the cost of living will double even more quickly.

There are two ways to handle the effects of inflation: You can live a less comfortable lifestyle or generate additional income. If you are retired and no longer being paid for work you do, the only way to increase your income is to be able to draw on the earnings in your investment portfolio. Ideally the earnings rate will exceed the rate of inflation.

Inflation Reality Check

(Chart showing income rising from $50,000 at age 60 to $100,000 by age 85, labeled "Current Income")

USING VARIABLE ANNUITIES

Having variable annuity income to supplement the money you need in retirement can help make long-term planning easier. Even though the amount of each payment may fluctuate, you can count on receiving income consistently. Perhaps more important, though, is that you can choose an option that will guarantee income for as long as you live.

And, with a variable annuity, you can spread your money around in a number of investment portfolios. That protects you from having all your eggs in one basket, and lets you share the benefit if investments in those portfolios grow in value or produce strong earnings, or both.

Making Your Money Last

One of the biggest challenges you'll face in retirement is managing your money so that it will last for the rest of your life. Here are some questions to consider as you make your plans:

1. What effect will taking money out of your various retirement accounts have on their continued ability to grow and provide income for as long as you live?

2. What part of your income can you count on and what part is less predictable?

3. How diversified are your income sources? Are you too vulnerable to major changes in the economy, including declining interest rates?

15

ANNUITIES

Immediate Annuity Income

There's nothing like an instant return to provide a sense of security.

Immediate annuities offer something no other retirement plans do: the opportunity to start receiving income right away. That's why they're sometimes described as payout annuities.

Since you buy an immediate annuity by paying a single premium, this type of annuity can be an attractive choice if you collect a one-time pension payout, sell a business, inherit money, or receive an insurance benefit and want to convert these assets to a source of regular future income.

What's more, you can purchase an immediate annuity and convert your cash to income at a time that suits you. That's one way they differ from a deferred annuity, which you should consider a long-term commitment to accumulating retirement assets.

LOOKING AT THE BENEFITS

You can set up your immediate annuity to receive income monthly, quarterly, semi-annually, or annually. That can be a big advantage over other income-producing investments such as bonds, which typically pay on a fixed, semi-annual schedule.

And remember that immediate annuities provide an additional benefit, since part of each income payment is return of principal on which you owe no tax.

One criticism sometimes levelled at fixed immediate annuities, and annuities in general, is that you lose access to and control over your assets. However, some immediate annuities let you commute your contract, which means you can accelerate your payments, or take some or all of the cash value minus expenses in a lump sum at any point.

FIXED INCOME

A **fixed immediate annuity** provides a steady, reliable stream of income for your lifetime, for two lifetimes, usually yours and your spouse's, or for a certain period of time. As with other annuities, the income you receive depends on the size of the premium, your age or joint ages, the interest rate, and the number of guarantees that are provided. For example, a payout guaranteed to last as long as you and your spouse are alive will provide a smaller payment than one paid solely for your lifetime.

One issue with this type of annuity is that fixed income is vulnerable to inflation, since the cost of living will most likely increase over your lifetime but the money you get from the annuity will not.

For some people, though, being assured that a specific amount will arrive on a regular basis is more appealing than having to take responsibility for managing their assets or worry about getting smaller payments in some periods. For example, a surviving spouse who inherits a substantial sum can avoid having to make investment decisions by converting the money to a fixed immediate annuity.

Remember that the older you are when the annuity begins, the higher the payment amount. That's because more of the principal is repaid each time.

WHERE THE MONEY GOES

When an annuitant dies sooner than expected, what happens to the assets that have accumulated in the annuity contract? If the payout is for a term certain, the beneficiary continues to receive income for that period. If it is a lifetime payout, the assets revert to the issuing company, where they are used to provide income payments to other annuitants who live longer than expected. In fact, the guarantee of lifetime income based on average life expectancy assumes that just as some people will live longer, others will die sooner.

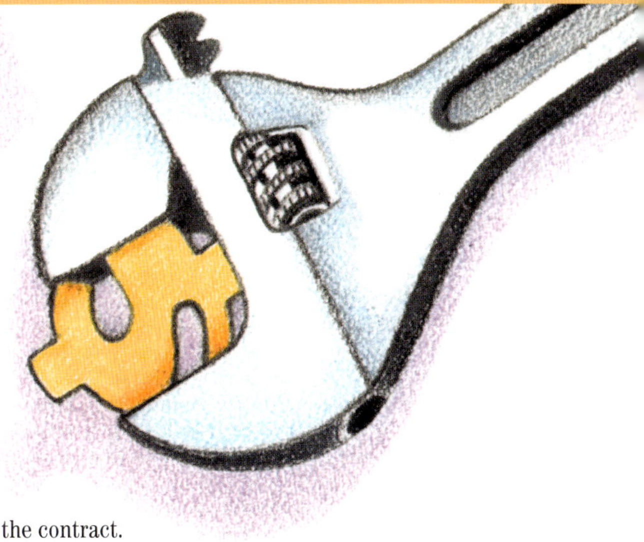

ANNUITIES

VARIABLE INCOME

Variable immediate annuities combine the assurance of regular income with the advantage of continuing to be invested in equity markets by choosing among those investment portfolios offered through the contract. That means the amount of income you receive may increase over time, so that you're in a better position to keep pace with or exceed the rate of inflation.

Of course the amount you receive may also decrease at any time if investment performance declines. Historically, however, the equity markets have been a good way to beat inflation over the long term.

Most variable immediate annuities offer the same types and varieties of investment accounts that deferred contracts provide. Most also allow you to choose the benchmark rate by which your portfolio's performance will be measured.

In an immediate annuity, the death benefit protection is in the form of continuing payments to your beneficiaries for a specified number of years or a cash refund of the unpaid contract value remaining at your death. These assurances offset the concern that the issuing company might not pay out all you have invested if you die sooner than you expected. But they do depend on the claims-paying ability of the annuity company.

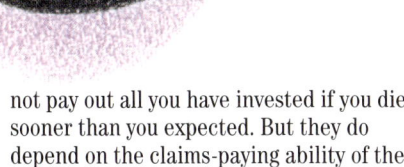

WHERE ANNUITIES FIT

Most experts suggest that an immediate fixed or variable annuity works best as part of a package that includes income from Social Security, your qualified retirement plans, IRAs, and your other investments. In that case, the lifetime income that an annuity provides may be an important factor in helping to ensure that you won't outlive your assets. Annuity income may also make you more comfortable about investing your other assets more aggressively.

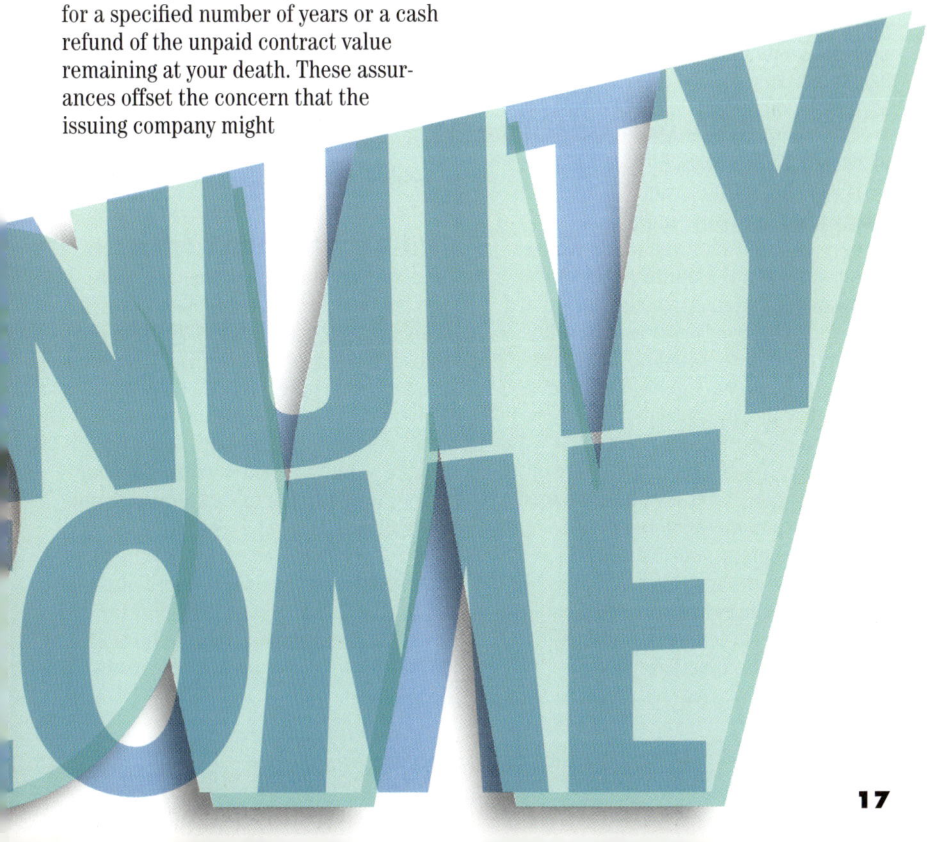

17

ANNUITIES

Understanding Variable Income

Variable income means the amount of your payments will change to reflect investment performance.

The point of choosing variable income is that if the value of the investment portfolios you have chosen in your annuity contract continues to grow during the payout period, the amount of income you receive may go up as well.

Of course, there's no way to project future performance, and your income could go down as well as up, especially in the short term. One benchmark is that between 1952 when variable annuities were introduced and 2003, large-company stocks provided positive returns in 39 years and negative returns in 13 years. For small company stocks, it was 37 and 15.

CHOOSING A RATE

As part of selecting a variable payout, you must generally choose among two or more assumed interest rates, or AIRs. That's a benchmark against which your actual investment performance will be compared after your income payments begin. Typically, companies offer AIRs that vary between one and a half and three percentage points. For example, AIRs of 3.5% and 5% may be offered by one annuity company, and AIRs of 3% and 6% by another.

If you choose the lower rate, you get a smaller initial income payment than you would with a higher rate. But the performance of your investment portfolios can meet or exceed the benchmark you've set more easily than if the AIR were higher. Each time performance minus expenses exceeds the benchmark, it can translate into larger payout amounts.

For example, if you choose a rate of 3% and the actual net gain in the value of your investment portfolios is five percentage points, your income will increase. But if you've chosen a 6% rate and the net gain is five percentage points, your income will decline even though there has been an increase in your account value.

ACCUMULATION PERIOD

Invested monthly	**$500**
Value of account at time of annuitization	**$100,000**

WHEN YOU ANNUITIZE

1. Account value is fixed at $100,000

2. Your present age and the AIR benchmark you've chosen determine how much per $1,000 in your account will be in your first payment

3. The number of thousands in account is multiplied by the rate

    100
   x $5.94

Your first monthly payment = **$594.00**

Rates for a Variable Annuity with Assumed Net Return Rate of

3.5% (AIR)

Amount of first monthly payment for each $1,000 after fees

Age of Annuitant	Amount per $1,000
63	5.63
64	5.78
65	5.94
66	6.11
67	6.29
68	

FINDING THE INITIAL PAYMENT

Once the benchmark has been set, you can compute the minimum amount you'll receive in your first payment by using the tables included in your contract. There's a different table for each of the AIRs and payment options the contract offers.

For example, assume you owned a variable annuity contract whose payment tables showed that a life annuity with an AIR of 3.5% would pay $5.94 for each $1,000 of accumulated contract value if you annuitized at age 65. If your contract was worth $100,000, your first monthly check (or direct deposit) would be $594 ($5.94 times 100, the number of 1,000s in $100,000).

ANNUITIES

ADDED APPEAL

Choosing variable lifetime income has a major advantage. In addition to money coming in on a regular basis, the income payments you receive may increase over time. In any period when equity investments are performing well—or what's known as a bull market—the amount you receive will tend to increase.

Once the amount you're receiving increases, any decreases in value are based on the most recent payments, not the amount of your first payment. For example, if over several years the amount you received increased from $267 to $400 and then values declined for a time, your payments might go down to $350 or even less. It is less likely, based on historical figures, that your payment amount will drop below $267, though in a serious downturn, or in a downturn occurring soon after your income stream began, it could.

> When the value of an annuity unit in your account goes up, your monthly payment increases. When the value decreases, the amount goes down for that period, but can go up again.

HOW VARIABLE INCOME WORKS

After the first payout, the amount you receive can go up or down depending on the performance of your investment portfolios. The first step in the process is to convert your first payment into a set number of **annuity units**. This is done by dividing the initial payment by the annuity unit value at the time of the payment. Then, this constant number of units is multiplied by the annuity unit value at the time of each future payment to determine the amount of that payout in dollars. Here's how it works:

STEP ONE: DETERMINING ANNUITY UNITS

In the example above, the first payment was $594. If the annuity unit value at the time of the payment was $10, you would be credited with 59.4 units (594 ÷ 10 = 59.4). The number of annuity units is then fixed so you always have the same number of annuity units as long as you continue to receive income.

STEP TWO: ASSESSING PORTFOLIO PERFORMANCE

Next, the company determines the value of an annuity unit for your next payment, which can increase or decrease based on the performance of your investment portfolios. If the net return on your investment portfolios is greater than the benchmark rate, the value of the annuity unit increases. If the net return is less than the benchmark, the value declines. For example, if the annual net return on your investment portfolio results in a 6.3% increase over the benchmark, the unit value would increase to $10.63 ($10 x 1.063).

STEP THREE: CALCULATING NEW INCOME AMOUNT

Finally, the company multiplies the new unit value times the number of annuity units to arrive at the amount of your payment. In this example, the new monthly payment would be $631.42 (59.4 x $10.63 = $631.42). Of course, the amount could go down as well as up in any given period.

ANNUITIES

Converting to Income

You need a plan to insure your income meets your needs.

Making the leap from deciding to take retirement income to putting that decision into action can be nerve-wracking. That's because the choices you make can mean a major difference in the way you live—sometimes for 30 years or more. And putting off decisions often seems easier than making them.

Realistically, though, you improve your chances of achieving the best results when you determine the income you'll need, weigh various ways it can be provided, and select the one that seems likely to best meet your needs.

WHAT THE ISSUES ARE
To make a strategic decision about the method you select to take income from your deferred or immediate annuity, it's smart to begin by analyzing what portion of your overall retirement income the annuity will provide. That makes it easier to determine:
- Your plans for the annuity income
- The right time to start getting that income
- The tax consequences of various ways of receiving the income
- How long you want the income to last

Make a Plan

PLANS FOR THE MONEY
The way you plan to use the money is often the key factor in choosing a payout method. So you should be aware of the advantages and drawbacks of your alternatives.

If you plan to make a large, one-time investment in the short term, you may decide that taking a full or partial **lump sum withdrawal** is preferable to choosing a gradual payout. You'll want to check your contract to see if there's a penalty or an extra fee if you choose not to convert the account value to a stream of income.

If you expect to use the extra income to supplement your budget or cover extraordinary expenses before you retire, **periodic** or **systematic withdrawals** may be the method you prefer. Systematic withdrawals let you receive income from the accumulated value of your contract on a regular schedule. You can adjust the amount or timing of the payments by notifying the company. Any earnings on amounts that remain in your account continue to accumulate tax deferred. But the income may not last for your lifetime.

Or, you can **annuitize** and convert your account value to a stream of income.

Pick the Right Time

SETTING THE TIME
There are some timing restrictions on withdrawing from a deferred annuity. Usually there's a 10% penalty if you take income before you turn 59½.

If your deferred annuity is part of a qualified plan or an IRA, you generally have to start by the time you reach age 70½. With nonqualified annuities, you've usually got another fifteen years or more before you must make a decision.

You can make an argument for postponing taking income until the last minute, especially if you seem to be managing without it. Then, when you do start, the amount you receive will be larger. For example, in some circumstances a person who begins taking income at age 85 might receive almost twice the amount in the initial payment as someone who began at age 62.

But there are often reasons for timing annuity payouts to begin when you retire, or even somewhat earlier. Annuities are designed to provide income for you, not to be left to your heirs—who may end up paying more in taxes than you would on the same income.

ANNUITIES

Personalized Plans

You may need more income early in your retirement than you will later on. And you may be more comfortable spending money on travel, for example, if you've deliberately created a stream of income designed to pay for it.

To be sure you have the money you want when you want it, you might ask your annuity provider about personalized payout plans or innovative programs for allocating your income. One strategy is to split your variable annuity payout into two streams, one to be paid out over your and your spouse's lifetimes and the other to be paid over five or ten years. For example, suppose you had a $300,000 annuity and allocated 75% ($225,000) to life income and 25% ($75,000) to a ten-year payout.

The amount you received during the shorter payout—perhaps $7,500 or more annually—could pay for extended travel or other things you've wanted to do. And since you'd planned the income specifically for that purpose, you could spend it with a clear conscience. At the same time, you'd be guaranteed income for life, based on the balance of the contract value.

CREATING A REVENUE STREAM

If you decide that the promise of income for life and the advantages of a regular return of nontaxable premiums as part of each income payment make sense for you, it's time for the next round of choices. The order in which you deal with them may vary, but these are the things you have to consider:

- Is the growth potential of variable income more important to your long-term plan than the predictability of stable fixed income?
- Would you prefer to have some variable income and some fixed income?
- If you choose variable income, which benchmark rate of return should you select, provided your annuity company provides a choice of rates?

FIVE YEAR PLANS

Since there's no way to be sure how long you'll live and need income, one approach is to make plans for five-year segments. That's long enough to see the effect of taking income from various sources during changing economic cycles. But it's short enough to catch potential problems and make adjustments in your spending style. This approach works well if you have the security of lifetime income for your basic needs.

Know the Tax Penalties

THE TAX CONSEQUENCES

You pay income tax at your regular rate on the taxable portion of your annuity income—on earnings only from a non-qualified annuity and on the entire amount from a qualified annuity or tax-deductible IRA. That's true even on the earnings that may have come from dividends paid on investments in your subaccounts or from capital gains from selling those investments.

If you annuitize a nonqualified contract, part of each payment is a tax-free return of principal until your total premium has been repaid. But if you take a partial lump-sum payout or arrange for systematic payments, the tax law assumes that you withdraw all of your earnings first and tap the principal only after you've used up the earnings. What that means is that you will pay more in taxes in the early years with these methods than if you had annuitized.

ANNUITIES

Annuitization Options

You can take annuity income in the way that suits you best.

When you buy an immediate annuity, or when you're ready to convert your deferred annuity into income, you will have to choose the way in which that income will be paid. Every contract offers a range of choices that provide different benefits, pay different amounts of income, and cover different periods of time.

WHAT YOUR OPTIONS ARE

While some contracts offer more income options than others, or use different language to describe your choices, you generally have six or seven alternatives, each with distinctive characteristics. You can get a good sense of how they differ by analyzing the information in the chart.

Payout option	How payout amount is determined
LIFE ANNUITY	Based on contract value, your age when payments begin, and interest rate (if fixed income) or investment performance and AIR (if variable income)
LIFE INCOME WITH PERIOD, OR TERM, CERTAIN	Based on contract value, your age when payments begin, interest rate (if fixed income) or investment performance and AIR (if variable income), and the length of the guarantee (typically from 5 to 20 years)
LIFE INCOME WITH REFUND PAYOUT	Based on contract value, your age when payments begin, interest rate (if fixed income) or investment performance and AIR (if variable income), and the refund guarantee
JOINT AND SURVIVOR LIFE ANNUITY	Based on contract value, your age and the age of your joint annuitant when payments begin, and interest rate (if fixed income) or investment performance and AIR (if variable income)
JOINT AND SURVIVOR ANNUITY WITH PERIOD CERTAIN	Based on contract value, your age and the age of your joint annuitant when payments begin, interest rate (if fixed income) or investment performance and AIR (if variable income), and the length of the guarantee (typically from 5 to 20 years)
FIXED AMOUNT (AVAILABLE ONLY WITH A FIXED INCOME PAYOUT)	You say how much income you want
FIXED PERIOD, OR TERM	Payment amount is determined by the length of time you choose to receive income, the contract value, interest rate (if fixed income) or investment performance and AIR (if variable income)

ANNUITIES

ALL IN THE TIMING

The income you receive from a deferred annuity when you annuitize depends on several factors, including the **contract value**, which is premiums plus earnings minus expenses, your age and the age of your joint annuitant if you have one, and the current state of the economy.

If interest rates are low, the income from a fixed annuity will be less than it would have been had rates been higher. You may want to consider postponing annuitization or converting only part of your contract value to income if it's possible.

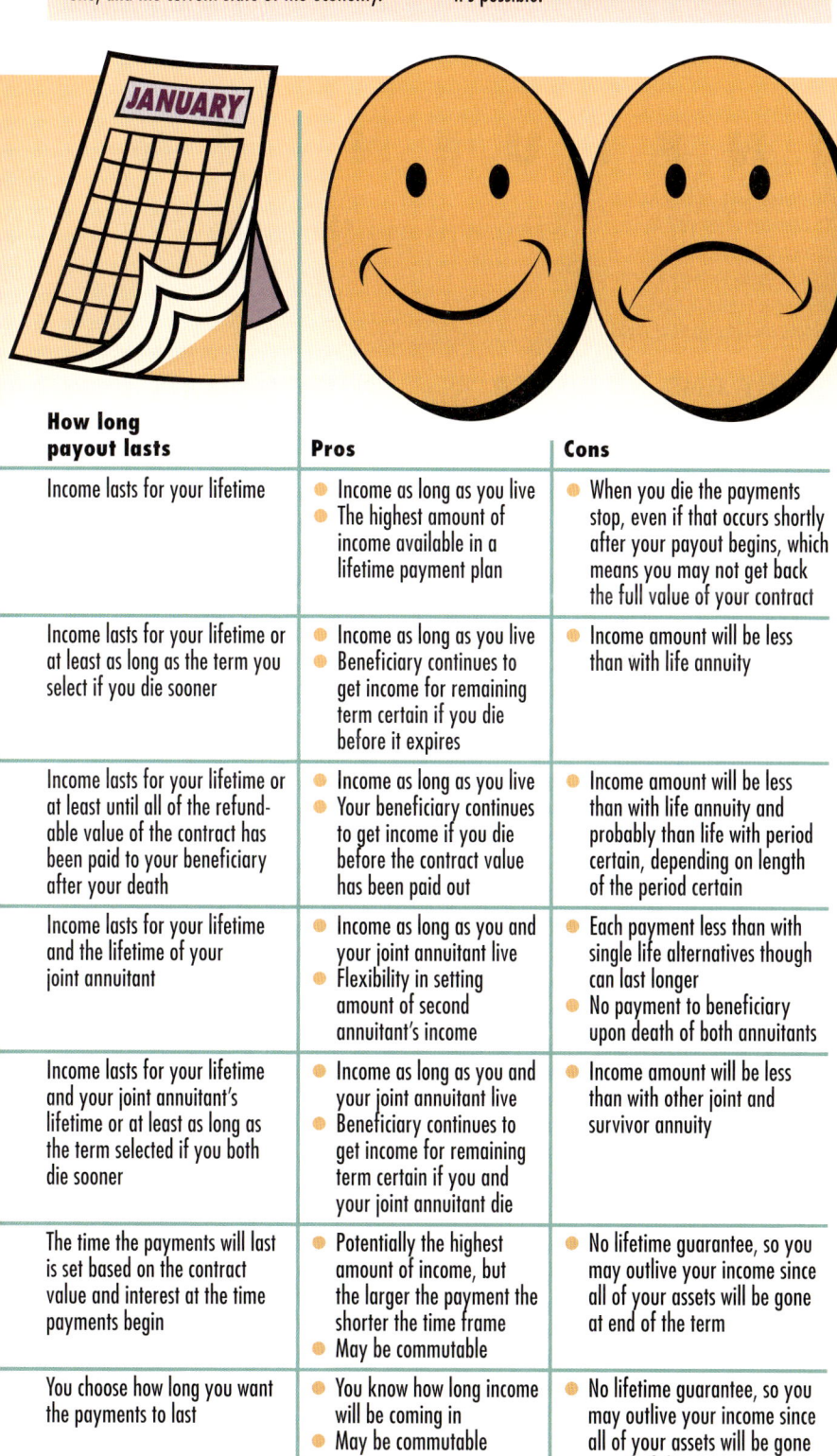

How long payout lasts	Pros	Cons
Income lasts for your lifetime	• Income as long as you live • The highest amount of income available in a lifetime payment plan	• When you die the payments stop, even if that occurs shortly after your payout begins, which means you may not get back the full value of your contract
Income lasts for your lifetime or at least as long as the term you select if you die sooner	• Income as long as you live • Beneficiary continues to get income for remaining term certain if you die before it expires	• Income amount will be less than with life annuity
Income lasts for your lifetime or at least until all of the refundable value of the contract has been paid to your beneficiary after your death	• Income as long as you live • Your beneficiary continues to get income if you die before the contract value has been paid out	• Income amount will be less than with life annuity and probably than life with period certain, depending on length of the period certain
Income lasts for your lifetime and the lifetime of your joint annuitant	• Income as long as you and your joint annuitant live • Flexibility in setting amount of second annuitant's income	• Each payment less than with single life alternatives though can last longer • No payment to beneficiary upon death of both annuitants
Income lasts for your lifetime and your joint annuitant's lifetime or at least as long as the term selected if you both die sooner	• Income as long as you and your joint annuitant live • Beneficiary continues to get income for remaining term certain if you and your joint annuitant die	• Income amount will be less than with other joint and survivor annuity
The time the payments will last is set based on the contract value and interest at the time payments begin	• Potentially the highest amount of income, but the larger the payment the shorter the time frame • May be commutable	• No lifetime guarantee, so you may outlive your income since all of your assets will be gone at end of the term
You choose how long you want the payments to last	• You know how long income will be coming in • May be commutable	• No lifetime guarantee, so you may outlive your income since all of your assets will be gone at end of the term

ANNUITIES

Annuitization Strategy

You can control the flow of retirement income.

If using annuity payments to provide lifetime income is the strategy that seems to make the most sense, you can select a payout plan that suits your individual situation. All nonqualified annuity contracts offer some tax-free income until the total amount of your premium has been repaid. All but two of them promise income for life.

INFLUENCING

There are several key factors to consider when you weigh the various payout options. It makes sense to review them with your financial adviser before making up your mind.

Who will get the money?

JOINT AND SURVIVOR

Should the payout be life only or joint and survivor? For many people, wanting to provide lifelong income for a spouse or other beneficiary is the driving force in choosing a joint and survivor payout. Each individual payment amount is less than with a single life annuity, but the total over two lifetimes can be more, sometimes much more.

SINGLE LIFE

When isn't a joint and survivor policy the wiser decision? Among the factors to consider are how much income each of you has from other sources and how healthy you are. For example, if you own an annuity and your spouse has a good defined benefit plan, taking a single life annuity might make sense. It would provide more income than a joint and survivor payout, and your spouse is already guaranteed lifetime income. Similarly, if your spouse is ill, and unlikely to outlive you, a single life annuity might be the wiser choice.

What percentage should the survivor get?

50% OR 100%

How much income should the survivor receive? The follow-up decision to choosing a joint and survivor payout is what percentage of the income that you receive while you're both alive should be paid to the surviving partner. There are usually several choices, with the least being 50% and the most 100%.

The decision involves trade-offs, as so many things do. If the surviving partner gets 100% of the income, the amount you get while you are both alive will be less. But the goal in choosing that alternative is that the survivor will have as much income as he or she needs.

On the other hand, a variable annuity paying the survivor 50% may provide sufficient income, since the living expenses of one person should be less than for two. Additionally, the variable annuity paying the survivor 50% may be able to provide enough growth to make up the difference over time if the investment portfolios you've chosen produce strong returns.

In one hypothetical example, a surviving spouse might receive an initial 50% payment of $228 following the annuitant's death. Some years later, the amount might climb back to $414, only $42 less than they had been receiving together. Of course, there is the equivalent potential for payments to decrease if the investment portfolios you've chosen do not produce strong returns.

ANNUITIES

THE FIXED ALTERNATIVE

There are circumstances when knowing exactly what you can count on each month may seem more appealing than the potential for growth.

You can get fixed income from your variable annuity by using either part or all of the accumulated value of your contract. The way it works is that the assets in your investment accounts are liquidated and deposited into the annuity provider's general account. The company then takes on the responsibility for making regular income payments.

With some contracts, you may also be able to choose a fixed payout that increases in increments of 1%, 2%, or 3%, reflecting increases in the cost of living. With this feature, your payments may initially be smaller than if you had not chosen increasing payments.

FACTORS

How long will you get the money?

PERIOD CERTAIN OR FIXED TERM

Should you choose a life annuity that guarantees a certain number of payments? One reason people give for choosing not to annuitize is that they're afraid if they die shortly after they begin receiving payments, they will forfeit a large portion of the amount they spent to purchase the annuity. To avoid that situation, some people choose a period certain payout guaranteeing that they or their beneficiaries will receive income for at least a minimum period, typically 5, 10, or 20 years.

You can choose a period certain payout whether you take a single life or joint and survivor option. Although the guarantee reduces the amount you get somewhat, most experts agree it provides added peace of mind.

Should you take a payout that doesn't guarantee life income? If the reason you're annuitizing is being able to count on income for as long as you live, you should choose the lifetime guarantee. But there are situations when getting a larger amount of money each month or ensuring payments will last a specific amount of time may be a better decision.

Some appealing features are that these payout models can produce the largest income payments in the short term. Also, when you select this option, you typically have the opportunity to **commute**, or cash in, your annuity for a lump sum rather than receive income payments in the future. In addition, in these plans part of your income payment is always tax free. With life payouts, you may end up owing tax on the entire income amount of each payout if you live long enough to have received your entire cost basis back. Of course, this isn't really a negative since it means that you're getting back more than you put in.

NOW AND LATER

What if you want to receive income payments while you continue to build your retirement assets?
A **split-funded annuity** lets you begin receiving income from a portion of your premium immediately while the rest of the money goes into a deferred annuity. The advantage is that you can get some income right away, while the balance compounds tax deferred. But remember that any deferred annuity is a long-term commitment. You'll want to ensure you're allowing enough time to realize gains.

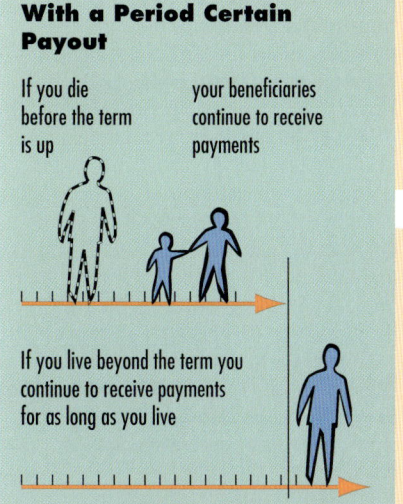

With a Period Certain Payout

If you die before the term is up your beneficiaries continue to receive payments

If you live beyond the term you continue to receive payments for as long as you live

25

ANNUITIES

What You Pay

There are some costs involved with owning variable annuities.

In addition to the premiums you pay to purchase an annuity, you pay ongoing fees to cover the services and benefits your contract provides and potential fees, such as **surrender charges**, which you may owe if you end your contract or withdraw within the first few years.

The amount you pay in fees and expenses varies, based on the type of annuity you buy, the company that issues it, and the specific terms that are part of your contract. For example, the way you allocate your variable annuity premium among the available investment options affects the amount you pay in fund expenses. Details of the charges that apply, how they're calculated, and when they're subtracted from your account value are included in the **prospectus** that you should read before purchasing an annuity.

In general, the fees for variable annuities are higher than those for fixed deferred or immediate annuities. The difference is based on the cost of providing the **guaranteed death benefit**, which is subject to the claims-paying ability of the issuer, the **investment portfolios**, **dollar cost averaging**, and the various payout options available when you annuitize.

FEE CATEGORIES

All annuity issuers charge you fees that cover overhead, sales and marketing, and the general cost of doing business. You also pay for the risks the issuer assumes, including the possibility that business costs might increase, that annuitants might outlive their life expectancies, or that investments the company makes to help meet their obligations provide disappointing returns.

You may also pay an **annual administrative fee**. Some contract providers waive the fee once the amount of premium you've paid reaches the required minimum, such as $50,000.

Asset-based fees are a percentage of the total value of your annuity, other than money allocated to a fixed account, deducted daily. All owners of the same contract pay the same percentage of their assets in these fees, but different dollar amounts. In some contracts, the rate drops as your account value increases.

You may also owe a transaction fee, sometimes called a **transfer processing fee**, if you make more transfers among your funds than the contract sets as the norm.

ANNUITIES

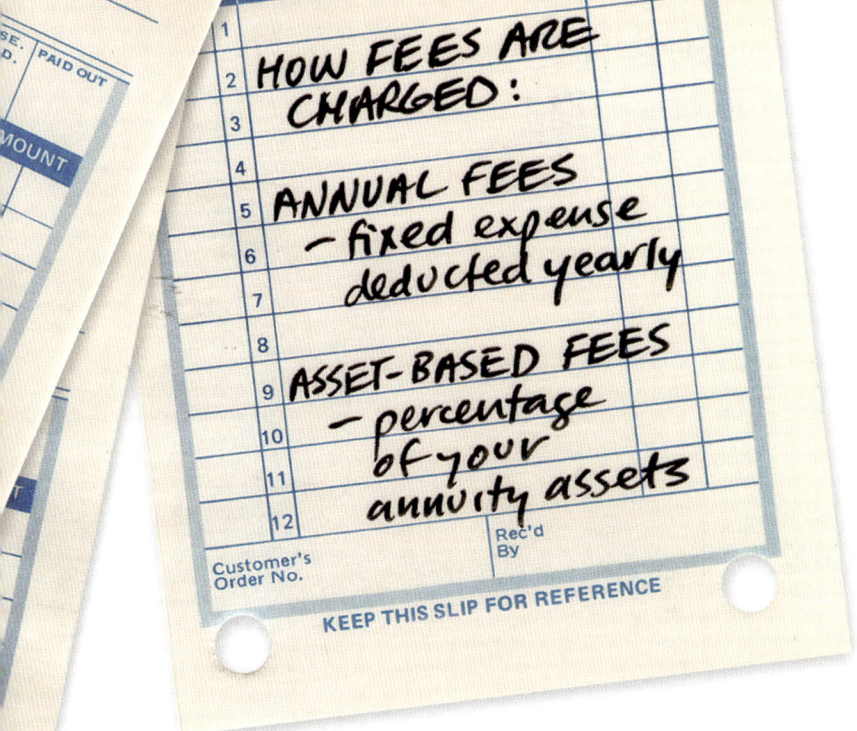

MORTALITY AND EXPENSE FEE

The asset-based **mortality and expense risk fee (M&E)** that is charged on all variable annuity contracts pays for four things:

1. The guaranteed death benefit
2. The option of a lifetime payout
3. The assurance of fixed insurance costs, including the M&E fee itself, which are frozen for the life of the contract
4. The guarantee of minimum annuity purchase rates when you annuitize

The cost of these **insurance features** averages 1.25% of the total value of your variable annuity each year. In most cases, the fee is subtracted proportionally from each of the variable portfolios into which you've put money.

When comparing a number of contracts, you'll find that sometimes the M&E fee is higher than average, while administrative and maintenance fees are lower, or vice versa. So you may want to look at the entire fee package, rather than any single component, in evaluating a contract.

MORE BENEFITS/MORE COST

A number of variable annuity contracts offer features often described as **enhanced benefits**. One example is a more generous death benefit guarantee, which locks in any portfolio gains for payment to your beneficiary should you die during the accumulation phase. Another benefit is additional protection for your income payments during retirement. These **guaranteed minimum income benefits** ensure a minimum lifetime income stream when you **annuitize**, or convert the savings in your annuity into income payments. Still other new features, such as long-term care protection, are also offered.

In general, you pay for these enhancements in additional fees. The fees generally reflect the nature and extent of the risks and expenses the company is assuming in providing these extra services.

STEPPED UP DEATH BENEFITS

Initially, the death benefit guarantee provided that your beneficiary would receive the greater of your contract value or the amount of your premium minus any fees and withdrawals if you died during the accumulation phase of your variable annuity. Today, some insurers have added new features to make their annuities more competitive and attractive. This means the cost of the death benefit feature may be higher. You have to decide whether the additional protection is worth the additional fee.

Remember too that collecting this benefit depends on the claims-paying ability of the company issuing the contract. Part of choosing an annuity provider should always include investigating the company's reputation and financial status.

ANNUITIES

More about Fees

There's a lot to be said for the concept of getting what you pay for.

Some fees pay directly for the insurance benefits that a variable annuity contract provides. Other fees pay for operating the individual investment portfolios.

MANAGEMENT FEES

Asset-based management fees are used to pay the investment portfolio manager as well as other expenses associated with operating a fund. These fees are described in the prospectus, and are sometimes broken down into an investment advisory fee and an operating expense fee. Other times, they're combined under the management fees heading. These fees don't appear as a separate figure on your regular statements. They are subtracted regularly from your account and reflected in your portfolio values.

The management fees vary from fund to fund within the same contract, based on who the advisers are and how the funds are invested. For example, fees on index portfolios tend to be significantly lower because the advisory costs are lower. On the other hand, fees on international equity portfolios or those requiring extensive research and oversight tend to be higher. This variation in the cost of owning different types of funds tends to be consistent from contract to contract, but the actual amount that you pay in management fees can be quite different from provider to provider.

If you put some of your money into a fixed account within your variable annuity contract, the expenses are paid by the account's **interest margin**. This margin is the difference between the percentage being earned on investments made by the company and the percentage being paid to you as earnings.

EXPENSE RATIOS

Another way to analyze the cost of an annuity contract is to look at its **expense ratio**. The expense ratio, expressed as a percentage of the contract value, can be found in the prospectus and is published regularly in performance reports that appear in the financial press.

The average expense ratio, including management and contract fees, but not sales charges or surrender fees, is 2.3%. You can check the expense ratio figures on your own, and you can also ask for that information from the insurance company or your financial adviser.

Even for portfolios offered by a single annuity contract, you'll notice that the difference in expense ratios can be significant. Those variations are the result of differing management expenses.

Though you probably won't want to choose your investment portfolios on

ANNUITIES

SURRENDER FEES

Most annuity contracts impose a charge or **surrender fee**, if you withdraw part or all of your contract value or if you terminate during the early years of the contract. These surrender fees are usually calculated as a percentage of the withdrawal and subtracted from your account value.

In most cases, the percentage you're charged declines each year. A typical contract carries a charge of 7% on withdrawals in the first contract year, dropping to 6% in the second year, 5% in the third, and so on, until it disappears entirely in the eighth year. The rates and the number of years the fees apply may vary from contract to contract. However, some contracts allow you to withdraw up to 10% or 15% of the contract value each year without penalty. With some contracts, the surrender fee period begins with the purchase of the contract. With others, a new surrender fee period begins with each new purchase payment.

Surrender fees benefit the insurance company that issues the annuity contract. The company has significant expenses for sales and marketing of the annuity, insurance underwriting, and other costs. So it counts on receiving asset-based fees or interest margin over a period of years. The surrender fees cover the loss of income that results when an annuity is ended earlier than projected.

There may be some ways to reduce or eliminate surrender fees, but there are tradeoffs. If you purchase Class A share annuities, you pay an upfront sales charge but no surrender fees. Fees for M&E are also lower than with traditional annuities, also called Class B shares. With Class L shares, there's a shorter surrender period but you usually pay higher M&E fees. Class C shares have no surrender period but also have higher fees.

HERE AND THERE

A few states impose a premium tax on amounts you use to purchase an annuity contract, whether you make a single payment or pay periodically. Those charges may be up to 4% of the premium, but more typically run around 2%. They're independent of any fees the insurer or management company charges.

In some cases, however, you may find that the way retirement income is taxed in those states that impose a premium can ultimately offset the added upfront cost of buying the annuity.

expense ratio alone, it should be one of the factors you consider, particularly when choosing among those with comparable performance records.

IS THERE AN AX TO GRIND?

Variable annuities are frequently criticized as more costly to own than other investments. The critics point out that mutual funds, which also involve asset-based fees, have expense ratios averaging 1.4%, in comparison to the 2.3% that's typical of variable annuities, based on data provided by Morningstar, Inc., and the National Association for Variable Annuities (NAVA). Those costs mean that an equity portfolio within an annuity contract must turn in a consistently stronger performance than a comparable mutual fund in order to provide the same level of return.

Those who argue that the advantages that variable annuities offer outweigh the added cost point to:

- The guaranteed death benefit
- The potential for a stream of lifetime income among other ways to receive income
- The opportunity for tax-deferred growth, which mutual funds provide only when they're held in an IRA or employer retirement plan

ANNUITIES

Taxing Annuity Income

The way you receive annuity income determines the tax you pay.

When you purchase an annuity, you postpone paying tax on your earnings until you begin receiving income from your contract. Then taxes are due on some or all of each payment. Figuring the amount you owe can be complicated, so it's wise to consult your tax adviser. You can also find information in IRS Publications 939 and 575.

TAXES ON ANNUITY INCOME

If you annuitize a nonqualified annuity, part of the income you receive is the return of your **cost basis**, or premium. The rest comes from your accumulated earnings. The portion that represents a return of your premium is tax free because you paid tax on that money before you bought your annuity. The balance, however, which is your earnings on the premium, is taxable.

If you receive periodic or systematic payments or make occasional withdrawals from your nonqualified deferred annuity during the accumulation phase, the tax law assumes you don't begin to get your premium back until you have received all of the earnings. That means all of your income is taxable in the early years of periodic withdrawals. In addition to the income tax, you may owe an additional 10% penalty if you're younger than 59½.

> **TAXING FACT**
> When you estimate the income you need in retirement, don't forget that you'll still owe income taxes.

If you take a lump sum, you owe tax plus the potential penalty on all of the earnings in the year you make the withdrawal.

With a **qualified annuity**, the total amount of each income payment you receive is generally taxable because you reduced your salary by the amount of the premium and paid less in taxes at the time you purchased or added to the contract. The same is true of an annuity you own in an IRA if you were entitled to a tax deduction for your contribution.

FINDING WHAT YOU OWE

When you receive nonqualified annuity income, you find the taxable portion by using an **exclusion ratio**.

FIXED ANNUITIES

With a fixed annuity, you divide the premiums paid for the annuity by the expected return, determined by IRS tables. The resulting fraction or percentage is the nontaxable portion of each payment until all of the investment amount has been returned. The balance is taxable.

$$\frac{\text{Premiums paid (Cost basis)}}{\text{Expected return}} = \text{Nontaxable portion of payments}$$

for example

For example, if you invested $100,000 in an annuity, and the expected total return is $250,000 based on your life expectancy and the interest rate being paid, you'd divide the investment total by the expected return:

$$\frac{\$100,000}{\$250,000} = 40\% \text{ Nontaxable portion of payments}$$

That means that 40% of the payments you receive in that year are free of tax, and 60% are taxed at your regular rate. So if you were getting $650 a month, you'd owe tax on $390 of it, or on $4,680 of your $7,800 annual income.

Monthly income	$	650
Percentage taxable	x	.60
Taxable income	= $	390
	x	12
Annual taxable income	= $	4,680

WHAT YOU PAY TAXES ON

	Nonqualified Annuities		Qualified Annuities
Payout	Cost Basis	Earnings	Cost Basis + Earnings
Annuitize	NO TAX	TAX	TAX
Periodic	NO TAX	TAX	TAX
Lump sum	NO TAX	TAX	TAX

ANNUITIES

VARIABLE ANNUITIES

With a variable annuity, the excluded amount is figured a little differently, since there is no way to predict the expected total return. Here, you divide your cost basis, or the amount you spent on premiums, by the number of years you expect payments to be made. In a fixed term contract, the number of years is the same as the fixed term. When you arrange for lifetime payment, you use your life expectancy depending on the payout option you choose to determine the number of years.

$$\frac{\text{Cost basis}}{\text{Number of years of expected payments}} = \text{Nontaxable portion of annual income}$$

for example

For example, if you had paid in $100,000 and your life expectancy was 20 years at the time you annuitized, the annual income you could exclude from taxes would be $5,000.

$$\frac{\$100,000}{20} = \$5,000 \text{ Nontaxable portion of annual income}$$

In this case, after you collected payments for 20 years, all of your income would become taxable.

BENEFICIARY TAXES

If you've started to collect income from your annuity, but die before all of the amount you're guaranteed has been paid, your beneficiary gets the remaining income. Those payments are free of income tax to the same extent they were free of income tax during your lifetime, and this continues until the value of the cost basis has been fully repaid. The remaining income is fully taxable.

If you die before you annuitize, your beneficiary gets the death benefit provided in the contract. The cost basis is returned tax free, and the balance is taxed in the manner which reflects the way it's received: lump sum, periodic payments within five years, or annuitization starting within one year after the date of your death. The payout method is determined by the terms of the contract and who the beneficiary is.

PREMATURE DISTRIBUTIONS

One of the limitations of tax-deferred investing is the 10% penalty on the taxable portion of withdrawals you make before you reach age 59½. Congress imposes this penalty to discourage you from touching your retirement money before you actually retire.

There are some exceptions for withdrawing from deferred annuities without federal tax penalty, though you do pay income tax on the taxable amount:

- You can withdraw if you are disabled
- You can annuitize for your life or joint lifetime, or set up a series of substantially equal periodic payments to last for your lifetime or the joint lifetimes of you and your spouse
- In certain circumstances with a qualified annuity contract, you can use a portion of your contract value to pay higher education expenses or buy a first home

The penalty doesn't apply to immediate annuity payments, which you can begin to receive at any age.

PAYING ESTIMATED TAXES

While you work, your employer typically withholds enough from your paycheck to cover the income taxes you owe. After you retire, however, it's your job to figure out—and prepay—the correct amount.

Generally, if you expect to owe at least $1,000, you must make quarterly estimated tax payments. Although annuity companies will withhold taxes from your income payments, you'll have to coordinate with the company to determine what you owe and to be sure the paperwork is in order.

GLOSSARY

Accumulation period is the time between your purchase of an annuity contract and the date on which you either annuitize or cash out your policy.

Accumulation units are the shares you own in variable annuity subaccounts during the period you save for retirement. As you pay additional premiums, you buy additional units.

Annuitant is the person who receives income from an annuity. You can be both the annuitant and the contract owner, or you can purchase an annuity to provide income to another person.

Annuitize means to convert the accumulated value of an annuity contract to a stream of income, either for one or more lifetimes or for a fixed period of time.

Annuity units are the number of units you own during the period that income is paid. The number of annuity units is fixed at the time you annuitize your contract and does not change.

Assumed interest rate (AIR) is the interest rate an annuity provider uses to determine the amount of each of your variable annuity income payments. The AIR is also known as the benchmark rate or the hurdle rate.

Contract value, also known as accumulated value, is the combined total of your principal and earnings in a variable annuity, up to and including the date on which you annuitize.

Expense ratio is the amount that you pay annually for the operating, management, and insurance expenses of your variable annuity, expressed as a percentage of your contract value.

Fixed annuity is a contract that guarantees you will earn at least a stated rate of interest during the accumulation period and that you will receive a fixed amount of income on a regular schedule when you annuitize.

Guaranteed death benefit is the assurance that your beneficiary will receive at least your principal and, in some variable annuity contracts, your locked-in earnings if you die during the accumulation period.

Immediate annuity is one that begins to pay you income within a short period of time, always less than 13 months. The annuity, which you buy with a lump sum, may be either fixed or variable.

Market value adjustment (MVA) is a fee you may pay if you surrender a fixed annuity or a fixed subaccount in a variable annuity. The MVA offsets any losses the insurance company might have if it sells assets to pay the amount due to you.

Nonqualified annuity is a contract you buy individually rather than through an employer sponsored retirement plan.

Premium is the amount you pay to buy an annuity or other insurance product. With a single premium annuity you pay just once, but with other types you make payments over time.

Principal is the amount of money you spend to purchase an annuity or other financial product. Principal is the base on which your earnings accumulate.

Qualified annuity is a contract you buy as part of an employer sponsored qualified retirement plan.

Subaccounts are funds made up of individual investments chosen by an investment manager. Each variable annuity contract offers a number of subaccounts, also known as investment portfolios or investment accounts.

Surrender period is the time between the date you purchase an annuity and the point at which no surrender fee would be due if you ended the agreement. In many contracts the surrender period is between seven and ten years, and the fee declines each year during the period and then disappears.

Tiered interest crediting means that an insurance company credits different interest rates to a fixed annuity's cash surrender value than it does to its annuitization value. Typically the rate is higher if you choose the annuititization option rather than taking a lump sum withdrawal.

Underlying investments are the stocks, bonds, or cash equivalents owned by the subaccounts of variable annuities or by other investment products, including mutual funds.

Unit value is the dollar value of a single accumulation or annuity unit. Unit value changes constantly to reflect the current combined total value of the underlying investments in your variable annuity subaccounts, minus expenses.

Variable annuity is a contract that allows you to allocate your premium among a number of subaccounts. Your contract value reflects the performance of the underlying investments held in those subaccounts, minus contract expenses.